W9-AVO-194

The SHOEMAKERS

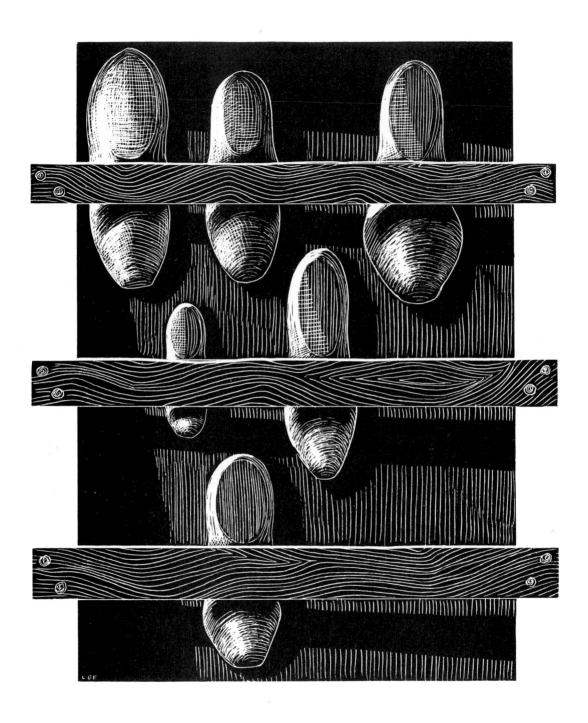

COLONIAL CRAFTSMEN

The
SHOEMAKERS

WRITTEN & ILLUSTRATED BY

Leonard Everett Fisher

BENCHMARK BOOKS

MARSHALL CAVENDISH
NEW YORK

Benchmark Books
Marshall Cavendish Corporation
99 White Plains Road
Tarrytown, New York 10591

Copyright © 1967 by Leonard Everett Fisher

First Marshall Cavendish edition 1998

Library of Congress Cataloging-in-Publication Data
Fisher, Leonard Everett.
The shoemakers / written & illustrated by Leonard Everett Fisher.
p.   cm. — (Colonial craftsmen)
Includes index.
Summary: Surveys the history and technique of shoemaking in colonial America.
ISBN 0-7614-0510-0
1. Shoemakers—United States—History—Juvenile literature. [1. Shoemakers.
2. United States—History—Colonial period, ca. 1600–1775.] I. Title.
II. Series: Fisher, Leonard Everett. Colonial American craftsmen.
HD8039.B72U66   1998   685'.31'00973—dc20   96-40975   CIP   AC

Printed and bound in the United States of America

1   3   5   6   4   2

Other titles in this series

════════

════════

A Short History

AS FAR AS IS KNOWN, THE CRAFT of shoemaking, or *cordwaining* as it was sometimes called, began on the North American continent in 1629. In that year Thomas Beard, a London shoemaker, arrived at Salem, the new Massachusetts Bay colony founded in 1628 by John Endicott and one hundred English settlers.

Thomas Beard was probably the first workman of his ancient craft to reach the English settlements. He knew that each of the Massachusetts Bay colonists had been provided with four pairs of "Well-Neat Leather shoes . . . to be good substantial over-leather of the best. . . ." But he also knew that the freezing winter snows and the mud, rain, swamps, underbrush, and hard, stony ground of the New England wilderness would quickly wear the strongest shoes and boots beyond repair.

To Thomas Beard, the prospect of doing a brisk business among his countrymen in a far-off, unknown land where he would be the only shoemaking craftsman seemed not a risk, but the opportunity of a lifetime. And so he not only

crossed the vast, dangerous ocean with his tools and all the leather he thought he would need, but he also brought his young apprentice, Isaac Rickman, with him. Beard worked at his craft in and around Salem for many years before moving to New Hampshire. Isaac Rickman returned to England as soon as he possibly could.

Soon after Thomas Beard came to America, other shoemakers and *cobblers*, those who mended shoes, began to arrive. These craftsmen traveled from house to house with their tools, making new shoes or mending old ones. The board and lodging they received while they worked for a family were figured as part of their pay. The leather they used was furnished either from their own supply or by the customer.

Because of their traveling ways the early American shoemakers and cobblers spread the latest news and rumors. In addition to their regular work, for which they were highly trained and well paid, they also often pulled teeth. This latter job was one that needed no special skill, but only a firm grip on a good pair of pliers, and a muscular arm to yank the bothersome tooth as quickly as possible.

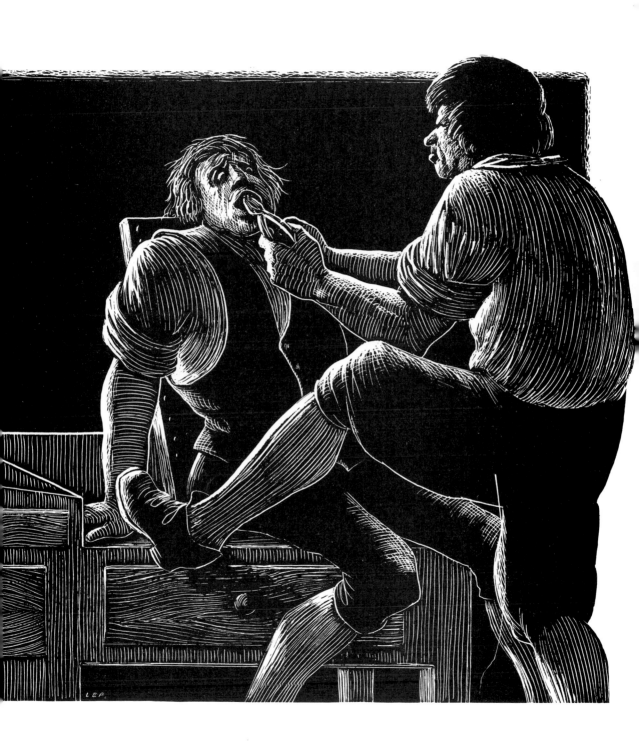

Between 1630 and 1633 there were not enough shoemakers in the Massachusetts Bay area to meet the great demand for their services. Many of the traveling shoemakers set up shop in their own homes in order to take on more work. Since more shoes were needed than they could possibly make, they began to charge outlandishly high prices.

Most of the colonists could neither afford the high prices nor wait out the weeks and months that would pass before their orders could be filled. Because of these difficulties, many of the colonists learned what they could from the shoemakers and made their own shoes. These shoes were uncomfortable and clumsy *straights*, shaped neither for the right nor the left foot.

Some parents apprenticed their sons to shoemakers, not only because the making of shoes was a promising line of work in early America, but also because in this way the whole family could obtain their shoes at reasonable prices.

Still, sturdy shoes and boots wore out faster than they could be replaced or properly repaired. They became so scarce in Massachusetts Bay Colony that large numbers of the settlers made

and wore Indian moccasins. During this time the public complained loudly about the shoe shortage and the high prices. The authorities could do little about the shortage except import shoes from England, and these the colonists could hardly afford. But the authorities did try to bring down the prices. In 1633 a law was passed that prohibited the Colonial shoemakers from charging more than a fixed amount of money for their work.

Meanwhile, Indian moccasins had become so popular that within a few years the colonists were exporting them to England as fast as they could be made. This scarcely pleased the shoemakers. For the next fifteen years they tried to form an association, or guild, to improve their lot and to get rid of unskilled workmen. But the authorities would not allow them to do this. Nevertheless, the shoemakers of Boston continued to press for the right to have a guild. In 1648 the "Company of Shoomakers," as they called themselves, won that right and were granted a charter.

By the end of the seventeenth century, great quantities of shoes were being made by the Boston "Company of Shoomakers." During the early part of the eighteenth century, however, Colonial

America's shoemaking center shifted from Boston to Lynn, a small town to the northeast. Here, in 1630, Francis Ingalls had established the first tannery, or leather-making factory, in America. During the years that followed, other tanneries were founded in and around Lynn. As time went on, several shoemakers opened shops there. They were near the tanneries, and the best available leather could be bought easily and quickly. The shoes made by the Lynn craftsmen were soon noted for their high quality.

In 1750, John Adam Dagyr opened a large shoemaking shop in Lynn. He employed numerous craftsmen and apprentices and specialized in women's shoes. These shoes were so well made that orders poured into the shop from all over New England, New York, and as far away as Philadelphia. By 1767, John Dagyr's shop was producing eighty thousand pairs of shoes a year. These shoes were the equal of any that were then being made in Europe and imported into the colonies.

Shoemakers and apprentices flocked to Lynn either to improve themselves or begin new careers. Many a shoemaker who learned his skill under

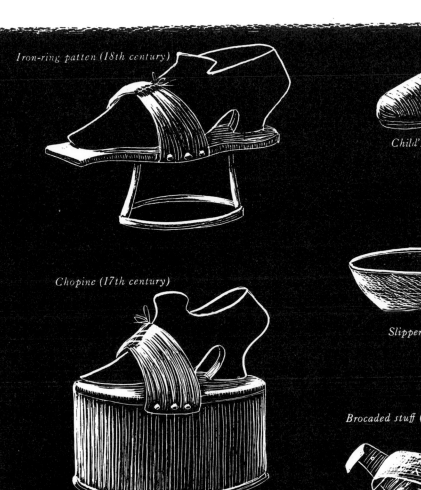

Iron-ring patten (18th century)

Chopine (17th century)

LEF

Child's clog (18th century)

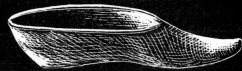

Slipper (18th century)

Brocaded stuff (cloth) shoe (18th century)

Galoe-shoe (18th century)

the watchful eyes of the Lynn craftsmen advertised this fact in the town or city where he later worked.

In the southern colonies of Maryland, Virginia, and the Carolinas, the situation was much different. Most of the wealthy plantation owners bought expensive footwear imported from England. Much of this imported footwear was made of cloth, or *stuff*.

At times, the plantation owners also imported leather shoes for their Negro slaves. And the owners who did not import their shoes had little need for traveling shoemakers. Some of them had slaves who could make shoes. If they did not have such slaves and did not import shoes, they either borrowed or hired a shoemaking slave from someone else. Or sometimes an owner had a white servant who had formerly been a shoemaker, and who was bound by contract to him for a term of years. This servant would be allowed to become a free man sooner than had been agreed to originally, provided he promised to make a pair of shoes for each of the slaves owned by his former master. Once freed, the servant returned to his old craft of shoemaking. When the job of making shoes for

The *HISTORY*

18

the slaves was done, he often found new customers. Or, more likely, he fell into debt and went to jail, only to be released as a servant under contract once again.

In any event, before 1750 hardly a shoemaker in the colonies made a pair of shoes unless they had been ordered to fit a particular customer. After 1750, during times when business was dull, the shoemakers began to make shoes of average sizes, but for no one in particular. These shoes were displayed in the shoemakers' shops for sale to anyone whose feet they might fit. Not until 1793 was North America's first retail shoe shop opened in Boston. Here shoes were not made, but only sold.

During the winter of 1777-78, George Washington's army of eleven thousand men camped at Valley Forge, Pennsylvania. There, on that hard and icy ground, more than two thousand American soldiers went barefoot. There were not enough shoemakers or materials to meet their needs. Yet the loyal men who lived through that terrible time fought on to free the nation.

How the
Shoemakers Worked

Metal hammer

Wooden mallet

Sole knife

Stretching pliers

Marking wheel

Burnisher

Awls

Size stick

S INCE, DURING COLONIAL TIMES, shoes were especially made to fit each buyer, the shoemaker's first job was to measure the feet of the customer. This was done with a *size stick*. Great care was taken to measure the length of the foot, but not its general shape or its width. These dimensions were merely noted by the shoemaker as being small, medium, or large. There were thirteen regular sizes for shoes then, just as there are today.

After the shoemaker had taken his measurements, he chose a wooden block of proper length and thickness. From this piece of solid wood he carefully carved a *last*, or form. It was a smoothly shaped model of one of the customer's feet. In Colonial times, shoemakers did not pay much attention to the differences in the curving of the left and right feet, and the same last was used for making both shoes. Therefore a shoe could be worn on either foot — on one foot one day, on the other foot the next day. This worked out well for those people who ordinarily would wear out one of a pair of shoes faster than the other. The shoes could be changed back and forth, and so wore more evenly.

A shoemaker's shop

The last itself was usually a bit longer than the customer's foot. That was ordinary practice in shoemaking, and was no problem. If the shoemaker had not correctly judged the small, medium, or large shape and width, however, his customer might have a great deal to complain about. Worse still would be a last with the wrong customer's name on it. Any mistake of judging the size, or any mix-up of customers' lasts, might result in shoes that did not fit at all.

Most of the ordinary people of Colonial times — men, women, and children alike — wore thick leather shoes with stubby leather heels and heavy soles. These boxy-looking shoes, called *batts*, first appeared in the colonies in 1636, when they were imported from England. At first, they were fastened to the wearer's feet by means of two straps, or *latchets*, which crisscrossed over the *tongue* of the shoe and were laced together with a leather string.

Although this style continued during most of the Colonial period, pinchbeck buckles were sometimes used in place of leather tie strings. The word "pinchbeck" came from a man named Christopher Pinchbeck, an English jeweler and clock-

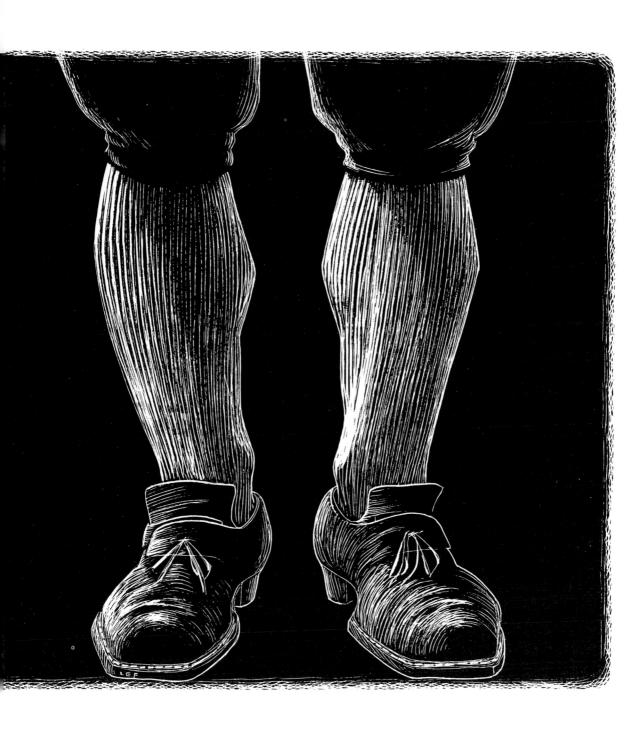

maker. In the early 1700's he put together about 85 parts of copper and 15 parts of zinc to make a new type of brass. Shortly thereafter, pinchbeck brass, plated with gold or silver, was used for shoe buckles. Most of these were made in and around Birmingham, England. The buckles were imported by the colonists, but the shoemakers hardly ever supplied them or even attached them to a shoe.

The shoe itself had three parts: *sole, heel,* and *uppers.* The soles were usually made of tough, thick cowhide. Sometimes they were built up in several layers, the outermost often being of wood. Such heavily soled shoes were considered work shoes or everyday shoes. At times, short, large-headed nails called *hobnails* were driven into the soles to keep them well joined and to prevent their wearing out too quickly.

The heel of the shoe was sometimes a thick block made of several layers of sole leather. Sometimes a solid block of wood was used instead, because it was cheaper than leather and lasted longer. Like the sole, the heel was often studded with hobnails.

The uppers were made of two pieces of coarse

Uppers

Sole　　　　　*Heel*

Hobnails

leather somewhat softer than that used for the sole. One piece, the *vamp,* covered the toe and the top of the foot, and ended at the ankle as the *tongue.* The other piece, the *counter,* covered the back and sides of the shoe, and came over the tongue in two crossing straps, or *latchets.* The counter of a more expensive pair of shoes was made in two pieces, sewed together in a seam straight up the back of the shoe.

All these parts had to be attached to each other and shaped over the last. The first step was to sew the counter to the vamp. When these two sections of the uppers had been joined, the shoemaker tacked them to the top edge of the wooden last. Next, he turned the last upside down and placed it in a *lasting jack,* which stood on the floor. The jack held the work firmly while the shoemaker used a pair of curved *stretching pliers* to pull the uppers up tightly over the sides of the last. As he worked he fastened the leather down with a second row of tacks at the bottom of the last.

When the uppers were in place, the shoemaker trimmed the extra leather to about one-half an inch from this second row of tacks.

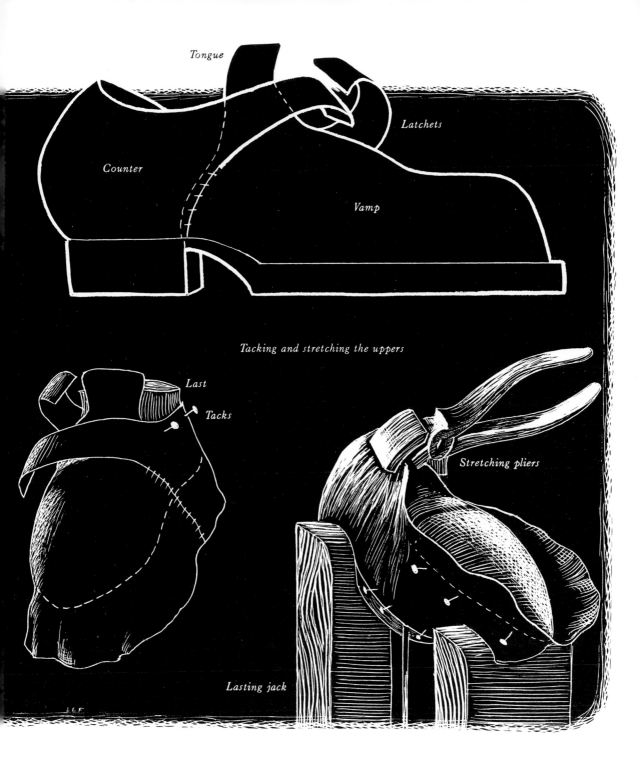

Tongue

Latchets

Counter

Vamp

Tacking and stretching the uppers

Last

Tacks

Stretching pliers

Lasting jack

Next he turned his attention to the sole. To make it soft and workable, the thick leather for this had been soaking in a bucket of water for many hours. When the shoemaker had removed the soggy leather from the water, he used his *sole knife* to cut it roughly into the shape he wanted. Then, sitting at his bench, he took up his *lapstone*, a smooth, flat stone that he held in his lap. Placing the sole leather on this stone, he pounded it with a metal hammer and a wooden mallet. This beating compressed the fibers of the leather and made it wear better. It also shaped the sole to the correct thickness. To keep the leather pliable as he worked, the shoemaker dipped it from time to time into the bucket of water.

When he was satisfied that the sole had been beaten enough, he was ready to attach it to the uppers. In starting, he formed a rim around the wooden last by bending out the extra one-half inch of leather on the uppers. Then he coated this rim with hot glue made from rabbits' skins, and placed the sole on top of it. When the glue cooled, it hardened into a solid film, strong enough to keep the sole in place on the rim of the uppers while the two were being sewn together.

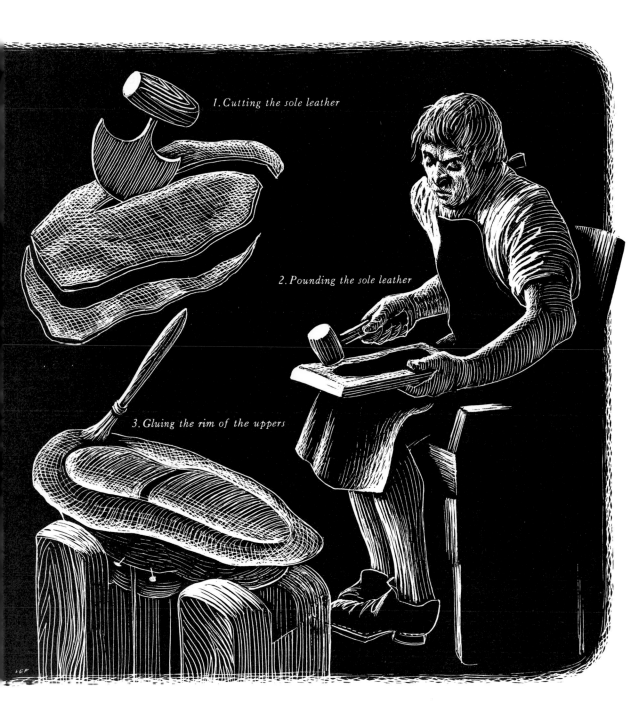

1. Cutting the sole leather

2. Pounding the sole leather

3. Gluing the rim of the uppers

Before he began to sew, the shoemaker cut a narrow groove, or *feather*, around the entire sole, close to its edge. He did this so that his stitches would not lie on the surface of the sole, where they would wear out quickly, but rather would lie below the surface. There they would be protected from constant rubbing against the ground, when a person walked.

After the feather was cut, the shoemaker ran a *marking wheel* along the groove, to mark off each point through which his needle and thread would pass. Next he used a sharply pointed *awl* to punch a hole at each of the marks he had made. Then he stitched the uppers and the sole together, using two strong linen threads smeared with beeswax and attached to two needles made of hogs' bristles. Each of the threads was passed through the same hole at the same time, but in opposite directions. This method of double sewing has come to be known as a *cobbler's stitch*.

If the man making the shoe was a farmer rather than a skilled shoemaking craftsman, he did not bother with feathers, marking wheels, waxed threads, and needles. He simply punched holes through the rim of the uppers and the sole, and

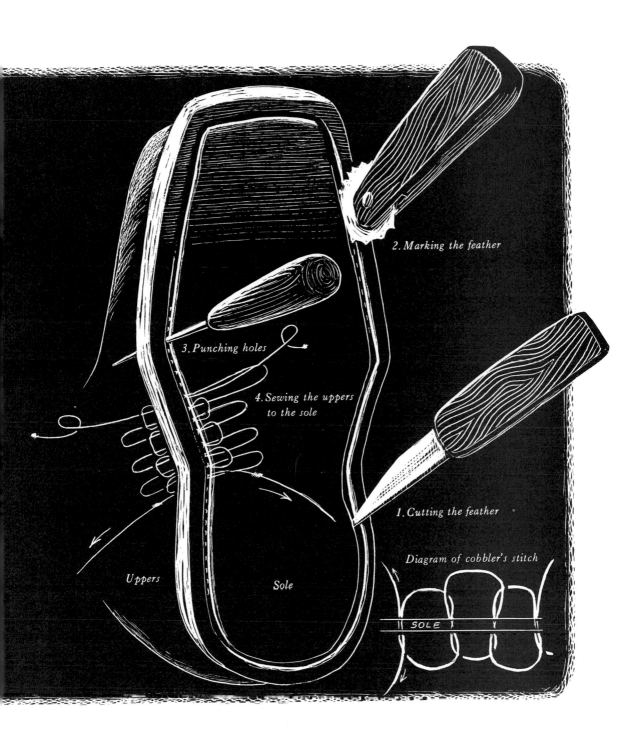

2. *Marking the feather*

3. *Punching holes*

4. *Sewing the uppers to the sole*

Uppers

Sole

1. *Cutting the feather*

Diagram of cobbler's stitch

SOLE

slammed tiny wooden maple pegs into them with one hammer stroke each.

After the sole and the uppers had been sewn together, the shoemaker nailed the heel in layers to the shoe and trimmed the sole evenly all round with a curved knife. He then removed the tacks that held the uppers to the wooden last, took the last out of the jack, and pulled the shoe from it. For the second shoe of the pair, he repeated the whole process. After this, the last was put away, not to be used again until that particular customer ordered more shoes.

Now the shoemaker punched two holes in each of the shoes' latchets for their tie strings. He used a scorching-hot iron to rub the heels and soles to a hard, glossy finish. If the newly made shoes were work shoes, he did nothing to change their dirty-brown color. He simply greased them with tallow. If the shoes were dress shoes, to be worn on important occasions, he stained the heels red and the rest of the shoes black. Red heels were first worn by the French nobility during the middle of the seventeenth century. They appeared in the colonies in the 1690's. For one hundred years thereafter, stylish Americans wore red heels.

1. Nailing the heel

2. Trimming the sole

3. Punching latchet holes

4. Burnishing the sole and heel

The work of the Colonial shoemaker was hard and slow. It roughened his hands and bent his back long before he became too old to carve a last. But the work did not dull his mind. It gave him plenty of time to think. Many a shoemaker, seated at his bench, pondered and spoke much about the times, boiling over as they were with ideas of revolt and independence. Shoemakers' shops everywhere became gathering places where people expressed opinions on many subjects. And as the voices in the shops rose about their ears the shoemakers "stuck to their lasts," making shoes for Americans who would soon walk in freedom.

Shoemakers' Terms

Awl — A tool used for punching holes in shoe leather.

Batts — Boxy-looking shoes that first appeared in the English colonies in the 1630's.

Burnisher — An iron tool which was heated and used to rub soles and heels to a gloss.

Chopine — A woman's overshoe having a stiltlike sole designed to increase the wearer's height or keep her feet from dirt and mud.

Clog — A heavy overshoe having a thick wooden sole.

Cobbler — A repairer of shoes.

Cobbler's Stitch — A method of sewing with two needles, used for attaching the sole of a shoe to the uppers.

Cordwaining — Shoemaking.

Counter — The part of the shoe that covers the back and sides of the foot.

FEATHER — A narrow groove cut close to the edge of the sole, to hold the stitching.

GALOE-SHOE — A clog, patten, or overshoe with a heavy sole.

LAPSTONE — A smooth, flat stone to be held in the shoemaker's lap while he pounded the leather of the sole.

LAST — A piece of solid wood, carved into a model of a customer's foot.

LASTING JACK — A vise for holding the last while the shoemaker worked on a shoe.

LATCHETS — Two straps, part of the counter, which crossed at the front of the foot, over the tongue, and were laced together with a leather string.

MARKING WHEEL — A wheel used to mark the points on the sole through which the needle should go.

PATTEN — A clog worn to increase the wearer's height or keep the foot out of the mud — usually worn by women.

PINCHBECK BUCKLES — Buckles made of a metal first compounded by Christopher Pinchbeck, English jeweler and clockmaker, in the 1700's, and made of 85 parts of copper to 15 parts of zinc.

SIZE STICK — A device for measuring the length of a customer's foot.

SOLE KNIFE — A knife for shaping the sole of a shoe.

STRAIGHTS — Shoes made in such a way that they were shaped for neither foot.

STRETCHING PLIERS — Pliers for pulling the leather of the upper part of the shoe tightly over the last.

STUFF — Cloth, sometimes used to make shoes.

UPPERS — The top part of the shoe, as distinguished from the heel and sole.

VAMP — The part of the shoe that covers the toes and top part of the foot.

Index

LEONARD EVERETT FISHER is a well-known author-artist whose books include *Alphabet Art, The Great Wall of China, The Tower of London, Marie Curie, Jason and the Golden Fleece, The Olympians, The ABC Exhibit, Sailboat Lost,* and many others.

Often honored for his contribution to children's literature, Mr. Fisher was the recipient of the 1989 Nonfiction Award presented by the *Washington Post* and the Children's Book Guild of Washington for the body of an author's work. In 1991, he received both the Catholic Library Association's Regina Medal and the University of Minnesota's Kerlan Award for the entire body of his work. Leonard Everett Fisher lives in Westport, Connecticut.